Why Stay Catholic?

ANSWERING COMMON OBJECTIONS

VOLUME I
MARY AND THE POPE

Adapted from the audio series by

DR. SCOTT HAHN, PH.D.

Edited by

DR. CAROL YOUNGER, ED.D.

Nihil obstat;
Reverend Harold Bumpis,
Censor Librorum, Diocese of St.Petersburg

Imprimatur:
Most reverend Robert N. Lynch
Bishop of St. Petersburg
May 19, 1997

The *nihil obstat* and *imprimatur* above were granted to the original transcripts of "Mary: Holy Mother" and "The Pope: Holy Father" printed in the "Catholic Adult Ed Programmed Study Guide" copyright ©1994 by St. Joseph Communications, Inc.

The *nihil obstat* and *imprimatur* are official declarations that a book or pamphlet is free of doctrinal or moral error. No implication is contained therein that those who have granted the *nihil obstat* and *imprimatur* agree with the contents, opinions or statements expressed.

Cover design by Devin Schadt
Saint Louis Creative
www.saintlouiscreative.com

Printed in Canada

Contents

Page

A Prayer to St. Joseph

O blessed Joseph,
faithful guardian of my Redeemer, Jesus Christ,

protector of thy chaste spouse,
the virgin Mother of God,

I choose thee this day
to be my special patron and advocate

and I firmly resolve
to honor thee all the days of my life.

Therefore, I humbly beseech thee
to receive me as thy client,

to instruct me in every doubt,
to comfort me in every affliction,

to obtain for me and for all,
the knowledge and love of the Heart of Jesus,

and finally to defend and protect me
at the hour of my death.

Amen

Why Stay Catholic?

At the turn of the 20th century, celebrated English author G. K. Chesterton shocked the public of his day when he came into the Catholic Church. Asked his reasons, he said there were ten thousand reasons to be Catholic, but they all reduced to one: Catholicism is True. After years of searching for the truth, Chesterton discovered that Catholicism was founded by the One Who is the Way, the Truth, and the Life.

Today, at the turn of the 21st century, non-Catholics are still investigating the Catholic faith. Like Chesterton, they are discovering that the Catholic faith is not only reasonable, but also practical, lived truth. And so, at a time when one would expect precisely the opposite, many Protestant ministers are embracing the Catholic Truth, often giving up their friends and careers to join the Church.

At the same time however, faithless priests, irreverent liturgies and other serious problems are tempting many Catholics to leave the Church. This series of books is dedicated to the many Catholics like you who are reading, studying and praying to support their Catholic beliefs and lifestyle.

Because the one reason for being a Catholic that Chesterton discovered is still the same: Catholicism is True.

Foreword

"Why do you stay Catholic?" I am one of the many thousands of Catholics who have been asked this question, although sometimes, it is an *un*spoken question. As I identify myself to my university students or to a new acquaintance, a sort of cloud of pity moves over the face of the listener. A kind of dismay that says: "Doesn't she know? It isn't politically wise to admit that you are a Catholic these days." How do you respond to such misguided consolers of your Catholic "condition"? And, believe me, you are definitely seen as having a Catholic *condition* rather than a Catholic *conviction*.

Well, I guess how you respond to the questions depends on your awareness of the power of, and rationale for, your Catholic faith. In other words, the real reasons for staying in the Church. If you are unable to explain <u>why</u> you believe <u>what</u> you believe, you might say, "Well, I was born into a Catholic family." Or even worse, make excuses, "Oh, I don't participate much anymore, since all this has happened."

Now, don't think I don't know we are in difficult times in the Church today. I know it is difficult to defend a Church that prefers the fluff of liturgical dances and theological innovation to the tough-minded living out of the morality of the Ten Commandments. And I know that there is a scourge of poor preaching and content-free educational programs for Catholic youth. Far too many of the few priests we have make themselves unavailable, and, lamentably, there are weak (even crim-

3

inally abusive) priests and bishops who promote immorality across our land by their scandalous lifestyles and heretical homilies and, worse yet, who neglect the sacramental care of the faithful.

But what would you say to someone who asked you, "Why stay American? The US has great sinners as citizens. Some of these sinners are even in its government!" Wouldn't you respond, "It's still the best country, and it's people are compassionate and heroic. Our history and our future are guided by the founding fathers and that guidance continues today. I wouldn't think of leaving America!" We Catholics have even greater reasons to "stay Catholic" than to stay American. We need to know our founding Father, and His Son, the great early statesmen (the Apostles), and the great events of the Church's founding (Salvation History in the Bible).

But there is more to staying Catholic than knowing the Church's founding people and events. Important dimensions of staying Catholic are presented in this short book that are crucial to Catholics, and are often the issues that cause confusion or argument between Catholics and members of other faiths.

First, there is Mary, the most important saint of those saved by Christ, saved before sin had any chance to touch her, so that her holy motherhood could carry us gently and tenderly to Jesus, her Son. Then there is the protection of papal primacy with its guarantee of true teaching on faith and morals without error, forever and ever.

These issues are among the "whys" of staying Catholic and are presented here in a commonsense, conversational style, designed for easy comprehension. Based upon Dr. Hahn's talks *Mary: Holy Mother* and *The Pope: Holy Father* from St. Joseph Communications' best-selling audio series *Answering Common Objections*, this little book explains how conflict over Catholic doctrines usually arises from a selective reading of Scripture. Now, thanks to Professor Hahn's clear teaching from a Biblical perspective, you will see the central treasures of the Catholic faith in their true scriptural settings.

A highly respected theologian, Scott Hahn converted to the Catholic faith after a soul-searching journey through the Bible using prayer and trust in Jesus as his guide. Now a professor at Franciscan University of Steubenville in Ohio, Hahn's depth of study and understanding of the Catholic faith have empowered him to present Catholic truth in a straightforward style, so that all listeners and readers can recognize, understand, and love the Faith. A popular speaker and teacher, his discussions within these pages will strengthen faithful members of the Catholic faith, while the many scriptural references will challenge "Bible Christians" to reexamine the Sacred text. And those who always wanted to know why Catholics are so, well, *Catholic*, will come to understand the loyalty that Catholics have to Jesus Christ, His Word in the Bible, and His Church. With this small book, you will discover crucial answers to the question, "Why stay Catholic?" And more-- you will be able to evangelize others, inviting them into the splendor and glory of becoming - and staying - *Catholic*.

Carol Younger, Ed.D.
October 2003

Part One: Mary, Holy Mother

The Book of Genesis and the Prophet Isaiah show that the role of Mary in salvation history was foreshadowed in the Old Testament.

Introduction

Where do we find in scripture the reflections, illustrations, assumptions and conclusions that the Catholic Church affirms with regard to the Blessed Virgin Mary? Scripture shows us Mary and the Marian doctrines. Briefly, we can look at some historical data, but our focus will be primarily scriptural. Now, non-Catholics are concerned with historical evidences for Marian doctrines and devotions. However, the vast majority of non-Catholic questions and objections to Catholic beliefs about Mary stem from scripture; specifically its seeming silence on the subject.

Scriptural View of Mary - Genesis 3

What scripture says about the Blessed Virgin Mary begins in Genesis 3. The first Eve was seduced and, I believe, brutally intimidated into disobedient submission.

Often we need to be able to read Hebrew to fully understand the temptation narrative. The literary artistry there is hard for the Western mind to appreciate. To sum up my understanding of the fall: Adam was called to be a faithful covenant head in a marital covenant, and he was called to show forth, as the representative of that covenant, the love, the *hessed*, the loyalty of the covenant to the fullest degree. And, as our Lord says, [John 15:12] *Greater love hath no man than to lay down his life for his beloved.* So, if he truly loves his covenant partner in marriage, he has to be willing to lay his life down. Now, God, the Father, tests his son's loyalty and love through the presence of the serpent in the garden. The serpent, *nahash* in Hebrew is misunderstood as "a snake." In both Medieval and modern artwork, Eve is depicted as some dumb woman. A little snake hanging from a branch in a tree tricks her into eating an apple from a tree. So all men congratulate themselves on being so worldly wise that they wouldn't be so dumb as this woman.

This misreads the narrative of the temptation. My own hypothesis, my own interpretation, is that *nahash*, the serpent, deliberately depicts a mythical, yet very real historical figure. Hebrew historical narrative often uses mythical imagery to communicate historical truth. For example, Daniel 7 describes four Gentile kingdoms as "four beasts." Similarly, in Genesis, the serpent is a dragon. The word is used repeatedly in Hebrew to indicate a dragon figure like Leviathan, Banmuth or Rehab, a monster elsewhere in the Old Testament. Revelation 12:9 confirms this translation of *nahash*, not as serpent/snake, but as serpent/dragon, because Satan is described as the *ancient serpent*, then describes a seven-headed dragon.

So Eve is confronted, brutally intimidated, by a dragon who is intent upon producing disobedience, come hell or high water. In the interrogation between them, Satan uses the truth in a clever, deceptive, but intimidating way to force Eve to sin: if she doesn't eat that fruit, she *will* die, at least in the biological, physical sense because Satan will see to it.

As you read, you ask, based not on anything explicitly stated, but rather on what is so conspicuously unstated, "where the heck is Adam in all this?" At the end of the narrative you discover he's right there by the woman, because she just turns and gives him the fruit to eat. The question remains: "where was he all along?" This loving covenant partner supposed to show great love and be willing to lay down his life for his beloved? Well, he probably rationalized his silence saying, "Well, if I oppose such a serpentile monster as this, I stand no chance."

Hebrews 2:14-16 tells us that Christ had to take on our flesh and blood to free us from the devil, from Satan, who held us in life-long bondage because of the fear of death and suffering we all have. So it seems as though Adam's response, or lack of response, is due to his fear of suffering and death, which in turn subjects all of *Adam*, humanity, to life-long bondage to Satan, who holds the power of death.

The first Eve is abandoned by her covenant husband, Adam, who was supposed to tell the dragon no and stand up for his convictions, possibly even suffer martyrdom laying down his life for his beloved, trusting that God, his Creator, to whom he is loyal in love would raise him up and vindicate him in proper covenant judgment. This is exactly what the second Adam does on behalf of the second Eve, the Church, which is the whole dramatic encounter we read about in Revelations 12. Mary, Ark of the Covenant, is the woman of the Apocalypse, who is clothed with the sun, a crown of 12 stars, and the world under her feet. She is the deliberate symbol of the second Eve for whom the second Adam lays down his life. Mary, the Church, Israel, and all New Testament believers are the covenant partner for whom Christ lays down His life and takes it up again.

To return to Genesis: having sinned, Adam and Eve were confronted by God. Genesis 3:8 *They heard the sound of the Lord God walking in the garden in the cool of the day and the man and his wife hid themselves.* This, too, is a mistranslation. With this translation there is a romantic, bucolic picture of God walk-

9

ing through the woods, with the sound of leaves crushing and twigs snapping as he says, "Adam, Eve, where are you?" Poor God, just doesn't really know what's going on! But the Hebrew, verse 8, says, "Then the man and his wife heard the sound of the Lord God." The same word in Hebrew for *sound* is used in Psalm 29, an entire psalm devoted to describing what Adam and Eve must have heard when they heard the sound of the Lord.

Psalm 29:1 *Ascribe to the Lord, O heavenly beings or sons of God. Ascribe to the Lord glory and strength. Ascribe to the Lord the glory of his name and worship the Lord in holy array. The sound of the Lord is upon the waters. The God of glory thunders. The Lord upon many waters. The sound of the Lord is powerful. The sound of the Lord is full of majesty. The sound of the Lord breaks the cedars. The Lord breaks the cedars of Lebanon. He makes Lebanon to skip like a calf in Sirion, like a young wild ox. The sound of the Lord flashes forth flames of fire. The sound of the Lord shakes the wilderness. The Lord shakes the wilderness of Kadesh. The sound of the Lord makes the oak trees to whirl and strips the forest bare and all in his temple cry, "glory"!*

What they heard wasn't the snapping of little twigs and the crunching of leaves. They heard a thunder and shattering roar, and they hid themselves, quite understandably. [Genesis 3:8] *They heard the sound of the Lord God as he was walking in the garden in the cool of the day.* In Hebrew, *cool* is *ruah*, normally translated *spirit* or *wind*, and that phrase could easily be translated as scholars have argued, *They heard the thundering, shattering roar of Yahweh Elohim as He was coming into the garden as the spirit of the day!* What <u>day</u>? The Day of Judgment, the *primo parousia*, the Second Coming in advance, in a sense.

So Adam and Eve flee from the sound, hiding from the Lord

10

God among the trees in the garden. [Verse 9] *But the Lord God called to the man, "Where are you?"* This is not about geographic location. God, the Divine, is omniscient. God knows where they are. Instead, He is asking, "Where are you in terms of your covenant standing before me. Where are you?" [Verse 10] *He answered, "I heard you in the garden, but I was afraid because I was naked and so I hid." "Who told you that you were naked? Have you eaten of the fruit that I told you not to eat?"* And what does Adam say? He immediately passes the buck. *The man said, "The woman you gave me gave me to eat."*

Adam's not just faulting her. He's implicitly blaming God. *And the Lord God said to the woman, "What is this that you've done?" The woman said, "The nahash deceived me and I ate."* Now, the serpent never actually lied, but he used a kind of blunt, brutal intimidation to get her to submit to the evil. *So the Lord said to the serpent, "Because you have done this, cursed are you above all the livestock, etc."*

But look at verse 15, *"And I will put enmity between you and the woman and between your seed and her seed. He will crush your head and you will strike his heel."* Now a scientist wonders: the serpent's seed, understood. But **her** seed? The Greek Old Testament translates this *spermatos*, the term for *seed*. What is it doing in connection with the woman? Nowhere else in the Old Testament is there an expression like that. It's always the man's seed, the husband's seed, the father's seed. The woman's seed? God will elevate the woman, giving her in a unique sense a seed through which the serpent's head will be crushed. This is a crucial passage.

Isaiah 7:14

The second most famous Old Testament passage for understanding Our Lady is Isaiah 7:14, an interesting episode between Isaiah and King Ahaz, King of Judah, who is worrying about the national stability of his people in Judah, his kingdom. He is surrounded by stronger neighbors, and he is toying with the idea of entering into the wrong alliances. Through Isaiah, the Lord says to doubting King Ahaz who fears his neighboring countries and wonders on whom he should rely   The Lord speaks through Isaiah, *"Ask of me and I will give you a sign."* In other words, your faith is weak. You need to be strengthened. Go ahead and ask me for a sign. With false modesty, Ahaz says, *"Oh, I won't ask. I will not put the Lord to the test."*   Isaiah replies, *"Hear now, you House of David, is it not enough to try the patience of men. Will you try the patience of my God also?"* In other words, God sees your need. He's got the gift that you need. Now don't play strong. You're weak. Admit it and receive the gift that he's got in this sign. *"Therefore, the Lord himself will give you a sign. The virgin will be with child and will give birth to a son and will call him Emmanuel."* The Hebrew word *almah*, translated by the Greek Septuagint as *parthenos*, has set off incredible debate. Is it "young woman" or is it "virgin?" I am persuaded, and not only by the Targums (ancient Jewish interpretation of Aramaic paraphrases) that the word means "virgin." Ancient Jews saw it as Messianic prophecy.

Other scholars debate about whether Targums were written before Christ or after Christ. There is evidence for both. However, Jews from earliest times saw a Messianic reference with regard to *parthenos*, a virgin. Professor Wyatt argues in an article that the Alexandrian Jews, who rendered *almah* by *parthenos* were being entirely faithful to the Herogamic tradition. He notes that Isaiah borrows all his pagan mythical imagery, then historicizes it with reference to the coming Messiah, in the ritual technical term for an embodiment of a divine mother, who is a fecund mother, a fruitful mother, as well as a perpetual virgin. In other words, Isaiah in using this language is tapping into a well-known ancient outlook on what humanity needs for deliverance, that is, God is going to have to send an incredible figure, the likes of which humans have never seen, a human creature, but also possessed by God in an absolutely unique way. And this, by the way, is not unique to the Hebrew tradition. It's shared throughout the ancient world. And that might be because Genesis 3:15 spread throughout the world as the human race spread. The fact remains that this translation of *almah* as *virgin* is strong, sure and very reliable. The New Testament applies this Scriptural passage to Mary and the virginal birth of Jesus. So Matthew's inspired Gospel narrative gives the "answer in the back of the book."

In Isaiah 7, the Davidic line is ending. The only way to keep it from ending, King Ahaz thinks, is to move away from Yahweh, to form alliances with all of these pagan neighbors. The problem is, in order to form those alliances, Ahaz must submit as a vassal to them. Isaiah says, "Don't do it. If you are weakening in your faith, ask God for a sign. God has one ready." As one of the faithful, Isaiah says "But God has sworn an oath: there will always be an heir on the Davidic throne." What happens if the king is deposed, and the royal family is murdered? Well, God will take a virgin and produce a son of David. In other words, God's children in covenant are not dependent exclusively upon human resources, political power, and economic wealth. So, Isaiah 7:14 stands in line with Genesis 3:15 as in a sense the second key text with regards to the Blessed Virgin Mary.

Mary as Ark of the Covenant

The Ark of the Covenant was the most sacred object in all ancient Israel. It made the Temple holy. It made the Holy of Holies the most holy thing in the world. However, it also was the most strategically powerful weapon that Israel possessed. Whenever Israel went to battle, the Ark led the way. When they encircled Jericho for six days, and on the seventh day blew the trumpet seven times, the Ark of the Covenant led the priests and the soldiers. The Ark of the Covenant is very significant. Most scholars say that it was a throne or seat, because many other ancient cultures had temples with arks. The unusual aspect of Israel's Ark was that it was empty. It was a throne with two cherubim over the top, but nobody sat on it. In fact, in the Ancient world, an ark was usually the throne for the Queen Mother. For instance, a great German scholar, in *Symbolism of the Biblical World*, speaks about the great popularity of cherubim thrones, box thrones with cherubim angels over top. He says that in Canaan and Phoenicia during the late Bronze and early Iron Ages, excavators describe an ark "as a female figure sitting in a square armchair." Odd? Why would these ancient cultures have an ark on which sat this female figure on kind of a throne posture? And why did they also just like Israel often lead that ark out into battle ahead of the troops? The common scholarly theory is that the woman was a kind of Queen Mother figure. Perhaps the thinking was: if your mother was out in the front lines, you might fight a little bit harder. So the Ark of the Covenant, God's presence among His people, was seen as producing all the miraculous victories. Jericho was the central stronghold of the Promised Land. It went down like a house of cards, with just marching the Ark around it seven times and the seven trumpets of the priests blowing.

Protestant, Lutheran, Presbyterian, and Anglican, as well as Catholic scholars, acknowledge that the New Testament deliberately depicts Mary in terms related to the Ark of the Covenant. And in Revelation 11:19, after 580 years without an Ark, Jewish Christians look up and see a sign. It is the Ark of the Covenant in heaven, which had not been seen in some 580 years. (This is where the title of the movie "Raiders of the Lost Ark" comes from.) Lost for that long, John sees it in Revelation up in heaven. And the very next thing he sees is [Revelation 12:1] *a woman clothed with the sun, with the moon under her feet, and on her head a crown of twelve stars*, a Queen Mother. The Ark is no longer an empty throne.

Mary as Queen Mother

Though we don't have the space here for all the Ark of the Covenant passages, there is a great deal of exciting, impressive evidence from the literary artistry of Hebrew narrative, preparing the way for the Davidic kingdom being fulfilled in the Son of David, Jesus Christ, with His Queen Mother, the Blessed Virgin Mary.

What do I mean by "Queen Mother?" This was one of the best-known institutions in ancient Israel's monarchy, and after the Civil War, in ancient Judah's monarchy. In fact, the idea of the Queen Mother was everywhere. All ancient monarchies in the Near East or the Middle East had Queen Mothers. A key article about this idea was written by N.A. Andreason ("The Role of the Queen Mother in Israelite Society," *Catholic Biblical Quarterly*, 1983, pages 179-194). The *gebirah* is the Hebrew term for the Queen Mother. *The Graphic History of the Jewish Heritage* states that the *gebirah*, the Queen Mother, "occupied a unique and powerful position" throughout the history of ancient Israel's monarchy. An example given is Bathsheba, Solomon's mother, enthroned by Solomon [1 Kings 2:19].

In fact, the northern kingdom of Israel was conspicuous because it lacked the Queen Mother. Father DeVoe, one of the greatest Old Testament scholars of the century said, "This was due to a lack of dynastic stability." They were overthrown repeatedly up north, not having the Davidic Covenant anchoring claims of their potential kings. A scholar in Scandinavia, Ostrum, says, "The Queen Mother's position was essentially cultic in nature." She had a position or a role to play in worship. It was not priestly, but it was important and it was cultic. The Queen Mother throughout all these ancient Near Eastern monarchies sat beside the king on a throne, and survived his death without being deposed. If the king died, the Queen Mother continued to reign without being deposed. There was a cultic role for her in leading the songs and so on in worship but also she had an essential role in political, military and economic affairs of court. In fact, there are records of where the Queen Mother could oppose the king on issues of state in the Eplah tablets and Ur Hittite records, Egypt Marri tablets, and Assyrian and other Arabian documents as well. An interesting incidental detail is that the Queen Mother usually began her reign after menopause. However, what is really interesting from Andreason's perspective is that, even after the prophets are sent by God to purify the Jerusalem cult and the kingdom of all of these pagan additions, the institution of the *gebirah* continues with reforms by Hezekiah and Josiah. The fertility cults are suppressed, *ashora* poles torn down, including sacred snakes, but never the Queen Mother. The central role for her is the king's wisdom counselor. Lady Wisdom in the Book of Proverbs is a personification of the Queen Mother, or vice versa.

Of the sixteen Queen Mothers named in this article, seven seem to be Jerusalemites. The tradition runs throughout the whole historical span of the Davidic monarchy. A Queen Mother, as instruction, wrote the only chapter of the Bible that we know was written by a woman, Proverbs 31, for her son before he accedes to the throne and finds himself a wife. Andreason concludes that "This is the theological paradigm for Mary's Queenship. Jesus is the Son of David, and the genealogy in Matthew links Mary to the Davidic line. Being the Son of David makes her the Queen Mother."

1 Kings 1: The missing link, the most important exegetical Biblical piece of evidence.

An example of the function and authority of the Queen Mother is in 1 Kings. Chapter 1 records the fraternal rivalry between Solomon and his half-brother, Adonijah. Adonijah is older, being born to one of David's wives whom he married before

Bathsheba. So Adonijah seemed to have a claim to the throne before Solomon, except that Bathsheba had exacted from David an oath to the effect that her son would get the throne.

First, King David asks Bathsheba, 1 Kings 1:16-18, *"What do you wish?" She said to him, "My Lord, you yourself swore to me your servant by the Lord your God, Solomon your son shall be king after me and he will sit on my throne. But now Adonijah has become king and you my Lord, the king, do not know about it."* The passage continues about Adonijah's palace coup attempt. Then King David calls Bathsheba. *So she came into the king's presence and stood before him. The king then took an oath, "as surely as the Lord lives,"* [1 Kings 1:28-30] David again swears *"Solomon, your son, shall be king after me and he will sit on my throne in my place,"* even though the majority of the people were going after Adonijah at the time, including several key priests. But Bathsheba rejoices.

Now, 1 Kings 2. David gives his royal charge to Solomon, and Solomon asks for wisdom as his kingly gift from God. What happens next is very unusual. Adonijah approaches Bathsheba in order to approach Solomon [Verse 13]. *Now Adonijah, the son of Haggith, went to Bathsheba, Solomon's mother. Bathsheba asked him, "Do you come peacefully?" He answered, "Yes, peacefully,"* then he added, *"I have something to say to you." "You may say it, she replied." "As you know,"* he said, *"the kingdom was mine. All Israel looked to me as their king. But then things changed and the kingdom has gone to my brother for it has come to him from the Lord. Now I have just one request to make of you. Do not refuse me." "You may make it," she said. So he continued, "Please ask King Solomon, he won't refuse you, to give me Abishag, the Shunamite as my wife."* If you understood palace politics, you'd see what this was. *"Very well," Bathsheba replied, "I will speak to the king for you."*

Abishag was David's last lover and wife, who kept him warm in his old age, sleeping next to him at all times. To have David's last wife would be an official claim to the throne. This is why Absolam publicly slept with David's concubines, after he threw his father out of Jerusalem. To have the Queen Mothers, to have the king's wives, is to be seen as the king. Solomon is no fool. When Bathsheba went to King Solomon to speak to him for Adonijah, see what happens. The king of Israel, the son of David, the supreme head of God's covenant people in the whole world according to Psalm 2, stood up to meet her, <u>bowed down to her</u> and sat down on his throne, and he <u>had a throne brought for the king's mother</u> and <u>she sat down at his right hand</u>. [Psalm 110:1] *Sit at my right hand*, the position of authority. Bathsheba says she has one small request. Solomon sees through it, says no, of course, and executes Adonijah. This is the beginning of the institution of the *gebirah*, something that continues. When the Queen Mother walks in, the king, because he is her son, pays filial homage to her and establishes her at his right hand, upon a throne as Queen Mother. That institution persisted down through the ages of the Judaite monarchy. There is no evidence of it ever being suppressed by the prophets, criticized by Yahweh, ever falling into hard times or being replaced because it had become meaningless.

After all this explanation, so what? So the Jews who had been waiting for 500 years for the Davidic line to be reestablished at the time of Christ's coming knew all this <u>well</u>. However, modern readers don't. Many Biblical scholars aren't aware of it. But every Jew was aware. God had sworn an oath that there would always be a Davidic king and that the kingdom of David would be restored in its former glory, even to greater glory.

For centuries, the Jewish people keep reading Psalm 2, Psalm 89, Psalm 110, Psalm 132 and other Davidic, Messianic psalms, promising an ongoing, unbroken line of Davidic succession with glorious power. Then Jesus is born.

Matthew 1

Those Jews who were expecting the Messiah, the poor, the humble, the faithful Jews, without political power or economic prosperity, who allowed themselves to be impoverished and oppressed, knew the Messiah would come and establish justice, not by force and violence but by an incredible act of self-sacrifice as both suffering servant and Son of Man. For them, Matthew 1 is the most exciting passage of the New Testament, though for us it is perhaps the most boring: the begats, the book of the genealogy of Jesus Christ, the son of David. However, the Jews would have gasped, "What? Can you prove that?" The son of Abraham! Abraham was the father of Isaac, Isaac the father of Jacob. Now, notice a few sections: in verse 3, Tamar; in verse 5, Rahab; in verse 5, Ruth; and in verse 6, *David was the father of Solomon by the wife of Uriah.* Four women are mentioned in this genealogy. It is very unusual to have women mentioned at all. But what do all four women have in common? Tamar had sex with her father-in-law; Rahab was a harlot; Ruth was a foreigner, a Moabite; and the wife of Uriah was just that, the wife of Uriah, before the wife of David, before he committed adultery and then committed murder to get rid of Uriah.

In other words, Matthew is reminding the Jews of the legacy of David's line. Why? Because what was the scuttlebutt about this young 13-year-old Jewess named Mary getting pregnant before she was married? Messing around, right? Whenever you see in the New Testament, Jesus called "the son of Mary," that's derogatory. Why? It was an illegitimate birth in the eyes of the townspeople, probably. What's Matthew doing? He is pointing out that the appearance of sexual immorality, or even the reality of infidelity, has never thwarted God's purposes. He uses as examples, Tamar's sex with her father-in-law, a harlot, a foreign

19

woman, and an adulteress. God's purposes had been fulfilled through the Davidic monarchy up until now, without God complaining about David coming from such women. And there was Solomon with his 700 wives, so this seeming scandal regarding Mary should not throw the faithful Jews off. [Verse 11] *Josiah the father of Jechoniah and his brothers at the time of the deportation of Babylon.* Then Matthew gives some good information that there is no absolute certainty about anywhere in the Old Testament. Jews didn't know what happened after Zerubbabel, and Matthew tells them. Abiud, Azor, Zadok, Achim, Eliud, Eleazar, Natthan, Jacob, then *Joseph, the husband of Mary of whom Jesus was born who is called the Christ.* In other words, Matthew says we didn't lose the line; God didn't forget.

What had been happening during all those centuries? If an heir in the Davidic line stood up and said, "Hey, I'm Davidic!", what would happen? The Babylonians, the Persians, the Greeks or the Romans would have killed him as a pretender to the throne. For the oppressors, this Davidic promise, this Davidic authority stuff, this "dynastic line" is over. So, those with royal blood, not just any old royal blood but divine right royal blood flowing through their veins, had better shut up. To illustrate: what happens as soon as the word gets out that the Messiah is born? What does King Herod do? He slaughters dozens, maybe hundreds, of infant Jewish males, no matter how diabolical an act, to put an end to the Davidic line. And Mary knew it all along. The Davidic line, as far as she is concerned, is found in the correlation of Mathaen and Lukan genealogies. God had not forgotten.

[Verse 18] *Now the birth of Jesus Christ took place in this way. When his mother Mary had been betrothed to Joseph, before they came together she was found to be with child of the Holy Spirit. And her husband Joseph, being a just man not wanting to put her to shame, resolved to divorce her quietly. But then the angel appears to him in a dream, "Joseph, son of David,..."*

20

In other words: "Now, Joe, remember who you are. You're a son of David. Weird things happen to Davidic sons. Okay?" [Verse 20] *"Joseph, son of David, don't fear to take Mary for your wife, for that which is conceived in her is of the Holy Spirit. She will bear a son and you shall call his name Jesus, for he will save his people from their sins." All this took place to fulfill what the Lord had spoken by the prophet: "Behold, a virgin shall conceive and bear a son and his name shall be called, God with us, Emmanuel."* Joseph probably knew this as well as he knew any verse in the Old Testament because this is one of those few key texts, those few key prophecies that *anawim* ("faithful remnant") held on to in hope. So *he knew her not until she had born a son and he called his name Jesus.*

Then, the Magi, sent by God, come to honor newborn Jesus. Matthew calls them Magi. Magi are Eastern Sorcerers, probably Persian. There's an old Rabbinic maxim, "If anybody learns anything from a Magi, one of the Magi, let him be accursed." They were the practitioners in the Black Arts. Some of the tools of their trade, according to Fr. Raymond Brown and other scholars, were gold, frankincense, and myrrh. They used gold for their magical pages on which the incantations were written, and they used frankincense and myrrh. When they present their gifts to our Lord in the manger, they are renouncing them. They have followed the light, found the truth. But of the most knowledgeable of the Jews? These, the priests in Jerusalem, are in the conspiracy with Herod, giving him all that he needs to track down the Messiah. Herod, the guy who kills his mother, kills his brothers, his cousins, who murdered 35 members of the Sanhedrin.

The Magi and the shepherds. In Luke, the shepherds also come to visit Jesus. The shepherds were regarded as the lowest part of Hebrew society. Women and especially shepherds were not allowed to give testimony in a courtroom. They were considered dishonest, perverted, according to Rabbinic sayings. This is like your neighbors looking out their window to see whores, junkies, and the pushers come to your front door to see your newborn baby. God has taken the humble and the sinners, those who are in most need of His mercy, giving them mercy and insight and wisdom. God turns upside down the wisdom and the power of this age and this world.

Luke 1

Luke is much less Jewish in his intentions than Matthew. Matthew wrote his gospel for the Jews and Jewish Christians. Luke is the only Gentile author of a New Testament book. He was a trained physician, a rather skilled historian, scholars tell us. He writes about Jesus, the Son of Man, Son of Adam. Matthew writes about Jesus, the Son of David. Luke is concerned in his genealogy to take Jesus all the way back to Adam - to show that this man is the one who is to redeem the whole world, all nations! After all, Luke is not a Jew.

Beginning in Luke 1:5, the annunciation to Zechariah and the birth of John the Baptist is recounted. After the birth of John the Baptist, the birth of Jesus is foretold in the annunciation [Verse 26]. *In the sixth month, the Angel Gabriel was sent from God to a city of Galilee named Nazareth to a virgin betrothed to a man whose name was Joseph of the house of David, and the virgin's name was Mary. And he came to her and said, 'Hail, full of grace.'* The Greek term for grace is translated variously, but the grace of God as it develops in the writing of the New Testament becomes a kind of substance, not just an attitude, not just a feeling or thought. Neither is it just a subjective posture or attitude. It's God's own life. So that when God favors you, He gives Himself to you.

So when Mary is full of God's favor, she is full of God's life:

that's the term grace in the New Testament. So, "Hail, full of grace, the Lord is with you" is an absolutely unique address. Never before has an angel addressed somebody almost *naming* them full of grace. It doesn't say, "Hail, Mary, full of grace." It says, "Hail, full of grace," saying it as a title. Scholars have torn this apart to show the distinctiveness and uniqueness of the address. "The Lord is with you." *She was greatly troubled at this saying and considered in her mind what sort of greeting this might be. "Don't be afraid, Mary," the angel said to her, "for you have found favor with God. And behold, you will conceive in your womb and bear a son, and you shall call his name Jesus. He will be great and will be called the son of the Most High and the Lord God will give to him the throne of his father David and he will reign over the house of Jacob forever and of his kingdom there will be no end." Mary said to the angel, "How shall this be since I have no husband?" And the angel said to her. "The Holy Spirit will come upon you, and the power of the Most High will overshadow you."* That word "overshadow" is a rare verb. It's used to describe the action of the Holy Spirit over the Ark of the Covenant. And so the connection with the Ark, a connection that is probably intended by Luke.

The Ark of the Covenant was so sacred because it contained the tablets of the Ten Commandments, the Decalogue, the word of God, the ten words of God. Mary is the Ark because the word has been made flesh, is dwelling *among* us, but *within* her. She is the true Ark, the true Ark of the Covenant, the New Covenant. Mary replies, *"Behold, I am the handmaid of the Lord. Let it be done unto me according to your word." And the angel departed from her.*

Mary makes haste to go visit cousin Elizabeth. As she walks into the house, John the Baptist "leaps for joy." Elizabeth says [Verse 43], *"Why is this granted me, that the mother of my Lord should come to me?"* Those who protest about the phrase *theotokos* or "mother of God" should see its Biblical precedent in Elizabeth's comment. *"For behold when the voice of your greeting came to my ears, the babe in my womb leaped for joy and blessed is she who believed that there would be a fulfillment of what was spoken to her from the Lord."*

And then, the song of Mary, the magnificent Magnificat! Built upon Hannah's song from the Old Testament, it goes far beyond that song in 1st Samuel. *"My soul magnifies the Lord and my spirit rejoices in God my Savior. For he has regarded the low estate of his handmaiden. For henceforth, behold all generations will call me blessed."* We usually think of Mary as humble, poor, faithful and so on -- and she is. Humility and modesty do not consist in making yourself into a doormat, however, or disowning God's graces and privileges. It means owning them as God's graces, privileges that are given to you to serve God and others. No false modesty for Mary. Mary knows her role. She is the Queen Mother of the Son of David, because she has been so humble and poor before the Lord. On her own she has nothing, but the Lord has filled her with everything. She says, "I am full of grace, but it's grace that I'm full of, not personal power or the ten secrets to success. It is God's grace, all gift, now mine so all generations shall call me blessed". The rosary just echoes the angel, "Hail Mary, full of grace. The Lord is with you." And then we say, "You are blessed amongst all women and blessed is the fruit of your womb, Jesus." Because God has done great things for Mary.

Luke 2:22 *And when the time came for their purification according to the law of Moses, they brought him up to Jerusalem to present him to the Lord. As it is written in the law of the Lord, every male that opens the womb shall be called holy to the Lord and offer sacrifice according to what is said in the law of the Lord, a pair of turtledoves, or two young pigeons.* This was the sacrifice for childbirth that was incumbent upon the poorest of the poor, for those who could not afford a real sacrifice, suggesting Mary truly was a handmaiden and Joseph humble and poor.

Luke 2:25 *Now there was a man in Jerusalem, whose name was Simeon, and this man was righteous and devout, looking for the consolation of Israel, and the Holy Spirit was upon him. And it had been revealed to him by the Holy Spirit that he should not see death before he had seen the Lord's Christ, the Lord's Messiah.* This passage shows that anybody full of the Spirit, meditating upon the Old Testament, would be expectant, waiting for a Messiah. *And inspired by the Spirit, he came into the temple. When the parents brought in the child Jesus to do for him according to the custom of the law, he took him up in his arms and blessed God and said, "Lord, now lettest thou thy servant depart in peace according to thy word for mine eyes have seen the salvation which thou hast prepared in the presence of all peoples. A light for revelation to the Gentiles and for glory to thy people Israel." And his father and his mother marveled at what was said about him. And Simeon blessed them and said to Mary, his mother, "Behold this child is set for the fall and the rising of many in Israel."*

These are not unmitigated blessings. The prophecy in Daniel 9 predicts the Temple will be re-consecrated, a strong covenant will be made, sacrifices shall cease, and the holy city will be completely destroyed and desolate. And so at the same time that the Christ comes to fulfill the prophecy after 490 years to re-consecrate the Temple, there is waiting to be fulfilled a doom pronounced upon those who have accumulated in Jerusalem wealth and political power, have corrupted the temple. Whose temple is it? Is it Solomon's? No, that one was destroyed. Is it the second temple that Ezra and Nehemiah helped rebuild? No, that too is gone. It's *Herod's* temple. He is a half-Jew Edomite who was murdering half his family. The downfall of those who wanted power and prosperity and wealth more than faith and love and grace and justice is imminent. [Luke 2:34] *A sign of contradiction and a sword will pierce through your own soul also, that the thoughts of many hearts will be revealed.*

John 2 --Wedding Feast at Cana

This is the first of the seven signs in the Book of Signs, the fourth Gospel. The first of Jesus' miracles is to turn water into wine just as the first miracle of Moses in Egypt was to turn water into blood. So, Jesus turns it into *the blood of the grape* [Genesis 49:11]. Here we have, I believe, something that is fraught with all kinds of rich literary and theological symbolism. [John 1:36] *Behold the Lamb of God* , says John the Baptist. In John 2, the Lamb goes up to a wedding feast. These two together should sound familiar: a wedding feast, a lamb in attendance. John is going to climax his book of *Revelation*, by inviting all of us to the wedding supper of the Lamb. And at the wedding banquet of the Lamb, we will meet a Virgin Mother in the Queen's city, the New Jerusalem, which is both virginally pure and maternally fruitful. Theologians have suggested that John deliberately loaded the first few chapters of his Gospel with symbolism and keys to interpreting his *Apocalypse*.

Mary approaches Jesus and says, *They have no wine* [John 2:3]. Jesus responds [Verse 4] *Woman, what have you do to with me?* A very interesting sentence. A top Biblical scholar in America, Manuel Miguens, wrote a study on the meaning of the Semitic idiom, "what to me and to you, woman?" He actually shows that there is nothing caustic or irritated about Jesus' reply at all. It's basically, "You know, there's nothing <u>between</u> you and me."

Jesus said to her, "Woman, what have you to do with me? My hour has not yet come." Jesus is thinking that the best wine will be given at "the hour." What does Mary say? Mary is assuming another posture, now. She distances herself from her son <u>as</u>

her son. Now he's addressing her not as *Mother*, but as *Woman*. It connotes Genesis 3:15 and other key passages of Old Testament scripture. Now with your request for wine, you are not just my mother anymore, what you ask in this miracle initiates a whole new economy of salvation, *Woman*. Mary becomes in this request a New Eve, a Mother to all of the renewed and redeemed humanity. *Woman, my hour has not yet come.* And Mary turns to the servants and says to them exactly what she says to us and all those who are truly devoted to our Lady, and through her to the Lord, *Do whatever he tells you.*

We should never allow ourselves to be so exclusively focused upon Mary that we don't hear her primary utterance. Do whatever *He* tells us! Marian devotion does not take us away from Christ. It refocuses our eyes and our ears on whatever he tells us because she is passionately concerned about now, as then, that we "Do whatever He tells us." Jesus tells the servants to take six stone jugs full of water, water that was used for the Jewish Rite of Purification to wash feet. Can you imagine, if you were one of those servants? Well, she said to do whatever he told me… and so, fill these big jars (hundreds of gallons of dirty water), then take that dirty, smelly water, used to wash feet and wash the dirt off people, from those same jugs, then fill the cups with this and hand it to the steward of the wedding. These servants don't know what to do with this man. What are they going to do when the steward of the wedding tastes the foot water? There's so much humor in this stuff that we miss. And they're saying, "We're going to get in trouble." "No, no," she said, "Do whatever he tells you." "We're just doing what the friend of the groom said, you know? We're just following orders, you know?" And then, [Verse 9] *the steward of the feast tasted the water now become wine and didn't know where it came from, though the servants who had drawn the water knew. The steward of the feast called the bridegroom and said to him, "Every man serves the good wine first, but when men have*

27

drunk freely and have become drunk, then the poor wine. But you have kept the best wine until now. This, the first of his signs, Jesus did at Cana in Galilee."

Now who is this steward of the feast who called the bridegroom? In John 3:27, this is what John the Baptist thinks about himself. *John answered, "No one can receive anything except what is given him from heaven. You yourselves bear me witness that I have said I am not the Christ but I have been sent before him. He who has the bride is the bridegroom, the friend of the bridegroom who stands and hears him rejoices greatly at the bridegroom's voice."* John the Evangelist has deliberately joined together what the steward at the feast, the friend of the bridegroom, has said about this great wine with John the Baptist, the last and the greatest of the Old Testament prophets who identifies himself as the friend of the bridegroom, the steward of the feast. The water in those six stone jugs goes back to Numbers 19 in the Old Testament. The water in the jars was for the Jewish Rite of Purification, for Jewish baptism purification. John the Baptist is using that kind of water to purify the people, getting them ready for the Messiah. That same kind of water is suddenly transformed into the best wine by the Lamb of God. John the Baptist is saying, "The New Covenant has come." In the *Apocalypse*, chapter 5, the Lamb of God is enthroned, leading all the people in worship, inviting all the universe to the wedding supper of the Lamb, where he presents the blood, the wine, the best of the New Covenant at his banquet.

This is what our Lady triggered with her statement. Though just a humble little Jewess, she knows what grace is all about. "Do whatever he tells you," and you won't even begin to anticipate the glories that will be revealed to you. If we will do whatever He tells us, we will not have to calculate what we can produce with our own human resources. If Mary tells us anything, she tells us that God can do the greatest things with the least things.

If we are tempted to say, "I'm really not that smart. I'm not that eloquent. I'm not that powerful. I'm not that rich. I'm a nobody." Then, bingo! You're qualified. You have just proven yourself to be the most qualified of all because whom does God love to use? The lowest, the least, the poorest, the humblest, the ones who know they are nobodies, so that when God does something great through them, everybody would look and say, "It had to be God." God gets all the glory. That is what Mary wants to do, to give God all the glory.

Conclusion: Why Give Glory to Mary?

Well then, why give glory and honor and devotion to Mary? Because we do whatever Jesus tells us. And we do whatever Jesus does. The fundamental axiom of Christian morality is the *imitacio Christi*, the imitation of Christ. He is the best of the best when it comes to being a son. Not only a Son of his heavenly Father, but a Son of his earthly mother, Mary. When he accepts the mission of his Father to become a man and to obey the law, he obeys it more perfectly than anybody could have ever imagined it being obeyed. He obeys the commandment, "Honor your father and your mother" better than any other son. That Hebrew word, "honor," *kabodah*, means to bestow glory. It comes from *kabod*, or weight, glory. So he honors his Father, and He obeys His Father's commandment by bestowing unprecedented glory upon the one that He has chosen from all eternity to be His Mother. The only time that the Creator created a human creature destined to be His own mother, He filled her with His own life and grace because He began honoring her as soon as she was created His Mother.

So what do we do? We honor Christ: we glorify Him, and we imitate Him. If we really imitate Him, we do what He does, honor and bestow glory upon His Mother. We do not do this *instead* of honoring Him. It does not *undermine* devotion to Christ. It expresses our devotion of Christ, our worship of

Christ, in imitation of Him. And if we do it we're going to be able to see in her the face of our mother, because Jesus has taken on her flesh and blood and given us His own Divine nature through her. Peter says, "*We are partakers of Divine nature through Christ*". So His Mother can become our Mother: spiritually, supernaturally, actually, and really. In devotion to Him, we can be devoted to her without any compromise, without any tug of war, without any lessening of our honor to Christ.

Love is not a finite substance. God is love. Love just keeps multiplying, reproducing itself. The more we love, the more love we have to give. 100 percent of our love goes to God and the God-man; therefore 100 percent of it and more is available for us to give to others, especially His Mother, who has become our Mother.

Jesus says at the Cross "to the disciple he loved," not "to John," "*Behold your Mother.*" Now which disciple did Jesus love? John as opposed to Peter? Not James, or Bartholomew? Jesus loved all his disciples then. He loves all His disciples now. Who is the beloved disciple who should look upon Mary as his Mother? All of us who are beloved disciples. In Revelation 12, *the woman gives birth to the male child who is to rule the nations, the Messiah against whom the dragon makes war.... The dragon makes war against the **rest** of her offspring, that is, on those who keep the commandments of God and bear testimony to Jesus.* They are beloved disciples. We are the brothers and sisters of Christ, the Firstborn among many brothers, and that makes us the children of the Queen Mother of the Son of David. The heavenly Temple is our home, the New Jerusalem our birthplace. The daughter Zion is our sister, and she is our mother, our bride, and our homeland.

Thank God that we don't have to undermine or take away anything from the glory of Christ. Rather, behold the ultimate masterpiece of Christ in Mary. Any artist, taking you into his room with all his masterpieces hanging on the walls, watches as you stand there staring <u>at them</u>, saying, "Oh my! You are such a great artist. You're fantastic!" He'd say in reply, "Hey, look at my <u>work</u>." He wouldn't feel offended if you went over to his greatest work and said, "This is awesome! Wow! Thank you!" He wouldn't say, "Hey, come on. Look at my face." No. Christ wants us to fall head over heels in love with His Mother because she is His masterpiece, His Exhibit A that He really accomplished salvation. She was saved from sin. That is why she is sinless. People are saved from sin *after* they sin, but Christ saved *her* from sin from beginning to end. She is the work of Christ, and we thank and praise our eldest Brother, our Lord, Master, our Redeemer, for His work in her, as we love and follow his Mother and "*Do whatever He tells you.*"

Part Two: The Pope, Holy Father

The Pope is a spiritual father appointed by Christ to care for the family of God on earth.

The Family of God

Many people think that Vatican II's vision of the Church was summarized in the phrase, "The People of God," but the Old Testament roots for that phrase, "People of God," "am' Yahweh" actually means "Family of God." That term "people," am', could be translated "kinsmen." So we look at the Pope, not as some tyrant, not as some authoritarian "know-it-all" or some magician who concocts revelation. He is a father figure whom Christ has established over the family that He purchased with His own blood.

People have many misconceptions. They sometimes think the Church teaches that the Pope is infallible, and therefore, he can't sin. That's nonsense. However, it is said that the present Pontiff (John Paul II) goes to confession at least once a week. He must have something to confess for Penance to be a valid sacrament administered to him. Others think that he always says the best thing at the right time. No, the Church has never insisted upon the fact that the Pope will always say the best thing at the right time. Rather, the teaching of the Church would allow for the Pope perhaps to postpone, out of cowardice, a right thing. Or when he says the truth, when he teaches the truth, he might do so in a way that includes an ambiguity. We need to understand, not only what the Church teaches but also what it <u>doesn't</u> teach, to correct misconceptions.

In simple summary, the Church teaches that the Holy Father, the Pope, the Bishop of Rome, as the successor to Peter and the Vicar of Christ, when he speaks as the <u>universal teacher</u> from the Chair of Peter in defining <u>faith and morals</u>, he does so with an infallible charism, or an infallible gift, through the Holy Spirit, so that we can give to him the full assent of our intellect and our will, and so that we can hear the voice of Christ coming to us through the voice of the Pope when he is speaking in this capacity.

There are three basic issues. First of all, proving Papal Primacy, that the Pope is not just the first among equals, but that he has a certain primacy, a unique supremacy in relation to all of the Bishops. We begin by showing that Jesus conferred this gift upon Peter. Secondly, we establish the doctrine of Papal Succession. Proving from the Bible that Jesus granted Peter a certain primacy, that doesn't go far enough. We then must establish Papal Succession; i. e., Peter had successors to whom would be entrusted the same gift (charism). Thirdly, we establish evidence for Papal Infallibility, that is: God grants a gift to the successors of Peter for them, not to give new revelations, but to preserve, transmit, explain, enforce public revelation. The Church insists that no Pope has ever given new revelation. Revelation has been, once and for all, deposited by Christ through His Apostles and, with the death of the last Apostle came the close of all public revelation. So the third doctrine is the doctrine of Papal Infallibility, that when popes transmit, when they explain, when they enforce, they are granted a charism or a special spiritual gift preserving them from error. Infallibility is a negative gift. It doesn't mean the pope always says the right thing, or it's always the right time to say it; but when he speaks with the authority that Christ gives to him, there is divine guarantee of truth. The Church of Christ is not a human institution first and foremost. Jesus identifies it as His own. The institution itself, and its up-building, Jesus claims for himself. "I will build my Church," Jesus says. So, the instruments Jesus chooses to use are under His control, and He uses them with the intention of building His Church, of governing His family. He ensures the guarantee He imparts in Matthew 16: the gates of hell will not prevail against the Church, nor against the Rock, Peter, and the Popes in the line of succession with Peter.

These are the critical <u>issues</u> regarding papal infallibility. Now, the key ideas to present as evidence and support for our belief and our practice as Catholics: first and primarily, Scripture, and also the historical development of the Church's understanding. Then, finally, Church teaching relative to the Pope and his authority.

Papal Primacy and Succession
Those three ideas are closely associated with the very important passage in the first gospel.

[Matthew 16:13 ff.] *Now when Jesus came into the district of Caesarea Philippi, He asked His disciples, "Who do men say that the Son of Man is?" And they said, "Some say John the Baptist, others say Elijah, others Jeremiah or one of the prophets." He said to them, "But who do you say that I am?" "Simon Peter replied, "You are the Christ, the Son of the Living God." And Jesus answered him, "Blessed are you Simon Bar-Jonah, for flesh and blood has not revealed this to you, but my Father who is in heaven; and I tell you, you are Peter* (Petra) *and on this Rock* (Petros), *I will build my Church and the gates of Hades shall not prevail against it. I will give you the keys of the kingdom of heaven, and whatever you bind on earth will have been bound in heaven and whatever you loose on earth will have been loosed in heaven." And then He strictly charged the disciples to tell no one that He was the Christ.*

Rather impressive testimony from the Apostles, because John the Baptist, Elijah and Jeremiah constitute the Old Testament Saints' Hall of Fame. As is characteristic throughout Matthew's Gospel, Peter speaks up. Peter is the only one to walk on water. Peter often speaks up, as representative of the twelve disciples. Peter calls Jesus the Christos, the Anointed One in Greek, or the Messiah in Hebrew.

A couple years before I became Catholic, I studied the doctrine of the Covenant. I came to an understanding of the Covenant as a family, and with this insight, I discovered all kinds of exciting truths, novel innovations, discoveries that I thought were really undiscovered before. Then as I began to dig deeper into these libraries, I noticed that time and time again, Catholic scholars - I mean not just recently but going all the way back to the 1st, 2nd, 3rd, 4th, 5th Centuries, in the Middle Ages - the saints and the Doctors of the Church had consistently come up with all of my brand new discoveries, teaching them with a kind of ho-hum attitude like, "You all know such and such." At first that provoked me. Then it scared me, and then it led me to dig deeper into Catholic sources. Those sources found practically every one of my discoveries, except the ones that were false. The Pope, though, was a different matter. For me, the idea of a Pope claiming primacy, succession and infallibility was presumptive, an arrogant presumption that no man should make.

But then one day, I was working through the Gospel of Matthew, because that gospel stresses and builds on the Old Testament more than any other Gospel. David's kingdom really seems to be the central thrust of Matthew's Gospel: Jesus is the Son of David and is establishing the Kingdom of David. That's how Matthew introduces Jesus. He is the only one of the four gospel writers who traces His genealogy right back to David, and he says, "Jesus, the Son of David" at the very start, continuing as a common and prominent theme.

In my study, I discovered first that in verse 17, *Jesus answered, "And blessed are you, Simon Bar-Jonah, for flesh and blood has not revealed this to you but my Father who is in heaven. And I tell you, you are Peter and on this rock I will build my Church."* All the evidence points to the fact that Peter is the "rock."

What's the excitement of that discovery? Well, non-Catholics frequently claim that it's Peter's faith that Jesus is speaking of, or Peter's confession that Jesus is speaking of when He says, "this rock." Or other Protestants object and say, "No, Jesus says, 'And you are petros.'" You are petros, you are rock, and on this petra, the Greek word for large rock, "I will build my Church." So some Protestants object to the Catholic view and say, "What Jesus is really saying is, 'You're a little pebble and on this rock, namely Christ, the Rock, (1 Corinthians, 10:4 and so on) I will build my Church.'" The closer I studied, the more I realized that those positions were simply untenable. In fact, the most conservative, anti-Catholic Protestant scholars today will admit that readily and candidly. The more I dug, the more I found that the evidence pointed to the fact that Jesus was speaking of Peter. Peter is the Rock. Peter just said, "You are the Christos," so Jesus says, "You are the Petros." There is a little parallelism there. "You are the Son of the Living God" and "You are the son of Jonah, Simon Bar-Jonah; you are the Petros."

People could say, "Wait a second. There is a distinction in the Greek language between petros, Peter's name and petra. Petros can mean stone, whereas petra can often mean 'big rock.'" The problem with that is two-fold. First, Jesus probably didn't speak Greek when He was with the disciples. This is held by 99.9 % of all scholars. It's unlikely that Jesus in His normal conversations spoke Greek. What's almost certain is that He spoke

Aramaic. In the Aramaic, there is only one word that could possibly be used. Kouman (and other scholars) have pointed to the fact that if Jesus spoke Aramaic, He only could have said, "You are Cephus, and on this Cephus I build my Church." So given our knowledge of the Aramaic language, there is no possibility for Jesus to have made the distinction between "little stone" and "big rock." The Aramaic language doesn't allow it.

Well, somebody could say, "The Holy Spirit inspired Matthew to use two different words." Well, that's true, because "petra" is the word in Greek that is normally used for "large rock," but - I should say petra is the Greek word that means "large rock" but it's in the feminine form. In other words, the gender of this Greek word, petra, large rock, is feminine. You do not apply a feminine form of the word in order to name a male. You adapt it by giving the masculine form. In other words, what Matthew was doing, guided by the Holy Spirit, is something that was rather obvious and practically necessary. That was to take the Greek from Jesus' saying and start by saying, "I will build my Church on this massive stone," this "petra" in the feminine but then to show that Peter gets the name, "Rock" in its proper masculine form.

You wouldn't name him Josephine or Rockina. You give Peter the masculine form of the word. I should also add that there is absolutely no archeological evidence from antiquity for anybody having been named Peter before Simon. In other words, Jesus takes a word that had never been used (as far as all the many records we have are concerned) to designate an individual person. And Jesus gives that name, that word, to Simon.

One of the greatest reformed Biblical scholars of this century, Herman Liderboss, a European scholar, in his Matthew commentary says, "The slight difference between these two words, petra and petros, has no special importance. The most likely explanation for the change from petros, Peter, masculine, to petra is that petra was the normal word for rock. Because the feminine ending of this noun made it unsuitable as a man's name, however, Simon was not called Petra but Petros. There is no good reason to think that Jesus switched from petros to petra to show that He was not speaking of the man Peter but of his confession as the foundation of the Church. The words 'on this rock,' petra, indeed, refer to Peter. Because of the revelation he had received and the confession it had motivated in him, Peter was appointed by Jesus to lay the foundation of the future Church."

Professor Donald Carson of the Trinity Evangelical Divinity School, an Evangelical, non-Catholic, American scholar, in *God With Us, Themes from Matthew*, says, "Jesus was simply using a pun to say that Peter is the rock on which Jesus would build His Church." Dr. Carson is not a Catholic Apologist. He would try to set up arguments against the Catholic faith, but he's sincere and respectable as a scholar in insisting upon obvious evidence.

So, Simon is the Rock. I have note cards that I put together when I was preparing a paper for a graduate seminar on the subject. I was still a Protestant minister, and I was taking a graduate seminar on the Gospel of Matthew and the professor was a Protestant. He was a Lutheran and he knew what I wanted to do for my project and so I presented this paper, "Peter and the Keys" and I worked at it because I knew that he might not be open to my conclusions, once I knew what my conclusions were going to be at the end of my research. They were rather Catholic, neither Presbyterian nor Lutheran.

So, I worked and worked, putting these note cards together, and I made the presentation. This was a very interesting experience, because for all the other students who presented papers, the professor encouraged the rest of the students to interact with the presenter. And he seldom, if ever asked questions in interacting. He wanted the students to get involved. But when it came to my 30-page paper presenting the evidence that Peter is the Rock and that the keys denote succession and that the Catholic position is right, not one student spoke up for the entire two and one-half hour seminar. He did all the talking and we even went over time. I ended up leaving the classroom like forty-five minutes after the seminar was supposed to end. It was the most grueling cross-examination I'd ever undergone.

But at the end of the whole ordeal he said, "I think your paper is flawless. The only fault that I found is that you have the middle initial on one person's name in one of your footnotes wrong!" He said, "I think your arguments are persuasive, too. I'm just grateful that I don't think that Matthew is historically reliable, so I don't have to follow the conclusions." What he meant was: I'm glad you said that, and not me.

Protestants are often ready to admit that Peter is the Rock and that the keys of succession are given to him to imply an office that will be filled by successors. For instance, one of the top evangelical New Testament scholars in the world, R. T. France says this in his commentary on Matthew, "Verses 17 through 19 are addressed to Peter and have been regarded by some as a late addition to support an early claim to the primacy of the Bishop of Rome. Whether or not they give any such support, there is no textual evidence for their addition to the gospel after its original composition, and the strongly Semitic or Jewish character of the language throughout these verses point to a relatively early origin in a Palestinian environment." What is France saying? Well, many scholars have suggested that Jesus could not have given this gift to Peter. Jesus could not have given this original saying. Why? Because many scholars don't believe that Jesus foresaw the building of the Church. They think that all of these sayings of Jesus concerning the Church were added later by the Church to support whatever had happened to the Church.

However, Dr. France says, "That's just not tenable." When you study this you realize that all of the evidence in the text shows that this is one of the original sayings of Jesus. He goes on to say, "Jesus' blessing is given to Peter alone. The other disciples may have shared his insight but Peter, characteristically, expressed it. Matthew often illustrates Peter's place at the head of the disciples' group. He was the spokesman, the pioneer, the natural leader." France goes on to say how Peter is referred to as the Rock. France says, "It describes not so much Peter's character that is the Rock. He did not prove to be rock-like in terms of stability or reliability but rather the name Rock or Peter points to his *function* as the foundation stone of Jesus' Church."

This non-Catholic, Evangelical Protestant, who has absolutely no interest in supporting the Church's claims, says, "The term Peter, Rock, points to Simon. Not to his character, because he could be very unstable, but rather to his official function as the foundation stone of Jesus' Church. The word-play is unmistakable." He says, "It is only Protestant over-reaction to the Roman Catholic claim, of course, which has no foundation in the text, that what is here said of Peter applies also to the later Bishops of Rome." In other words France is saying, "We can't apply this to the Popes, the later Bishops of Rome." (This objection is discussed below). However, France is very candid in saying, "Look, it's only because we Protestants have over-reacted to the Catholic Church that we are not frank and sincere in admitting that Peter is the Rock. He is the foundation stone upon which Jesus is going to build the Church."

One of the greatest Protestant Biblical scholars of the century supports this. W. F. Albright, in his *Anchor Bible Commentary on Matthew*, writes: "Peter as the Rock will be the foundation of the future community, the church. Jesus here uses Aramaic, and the only Aramaic word that would serve His purpose. In view of the background in verse 19, one must dismiss as confessional interpretation any attempt to see this rock as the faith or the confession of Peter." In other words, Professor Albright admits as a Protestant that there is a bias in Protestant anti-Catholic interpreters who try to make Jesus' reference to the rock point only to Peter's faith or confession. "To deny the pre-eminent position of Peter," Albright says, "among the disciples or in the early Christian community is a denial of the evidence. The interest in Peter's failures and vacillations does not detract from this pre-eminence; rather it emphasizes it. Had Peter been a lesser figure, his behavior would have been of far less consequence. Precisely because Peter is pre-eminent and is the foundation stone of the Church, his mistakes are in a sense so important, but his mistakes never correspond to his teachings as the Prince of the Apostles."

Albright goes on to speak about the keys of the kingdom that Jesus entrusted to Peter. Here's what he says, "Isaiah 22, verse 15, undoubtedly lies behind this saying of Jesus. The keys are the symbol of authority and Father Roland DeVoe rightly sees here the same authority vested in the vicar, the master of the house, the chamberlain of the royal household in ancient Israel. In Isaiah 22, Eliakim is described as having the same authority." Now what is he talking about? Albright is saying Jesus, in giving to Peter not only a new name, Rock, but in entrusting to Simon the keys of the kingdom, is borrowing a phrase from Isaiah 22. He's quoting an extremely well known verse in the Old Testament. This is the most important discovery of all. What was Jesus doing when He entrusted to Peter the keys of the kingdom?

By the way, there are hardly any Catholic defenders of the Faith today with awareness of this particular point. It is a point that defenders of Catholic faith in the 16th and 17th Centuries were very aware of. In Isaiah 22:19-20 ff, there is very interesting background. Jesus cites this passage:

[Isaiah 22:19] *I will thrust you from your office and you will be cast down from your station and on that day I will call my servant Eliakim, the son of Hilkiah, and I will clothe him with your robe and will bind your girdle on him and will commit your authority to his hand, and he shall be a father to the inhabitants of Jerusalem and to the House of Judah; and I will place on his shoulder the key of the House of David.*

Now the House of David is a dynastic reference. The House of David is the Davidic kingdom, the Davidic dynasty. We know this because David has been dead for hundreds of years at this point in Isaiah 22. *I will give you the key of the House of David. He shall open and none shall shut, and he shall shut and none shall open. He will become a throne of honor to his father's house.* Look at all of the symbols of dynastic authority that are given: (1) an office, (2) a robe, (3) a throne, and (4) keys, the royal key of the House of David.

Let me summarize in rather simple terms. Hezekiah was, at the time, the king over Israel. He was in the line of David hundreds of years after David, and ruler over the House of David. Now all kings in the ancient world had a cabinet of royal ministers. Hezekiah, as King, had as his Prime Minister Shebna, who proved unworthy. So he was expelled. Not only was there dynastic succession for the king, but also for the Prime Minister. When Shebna is expelled, Eliakim is called to fill the empty office. We know that Eliakim is now being granted the Prime Minister's position because he is given what the other ministers do not have, the keys of the kingdom, the key to the House of David that symbolized dynastic authority entrusted to the Prime

Minister and dynastic succession. Why does it symbolize that? Because it's the key of <u>David</u> of the House of David.

Let's read the quote from Albright: "In commenting upon Matthew 16 and Jesus giving to Peter the keys of the kingdom, Isaiah 22:15 ff. undoubtedly lies behind this saying." Albright, a Protestant, insists that it's undoubtable that Jesus is citing Isaiah 22, "The keys are the symbol of authority and DeVoe rightly sees here the same authority as that vested in the vicar, the master of the house, the chamberlain of the royal household of ancient Israel." In other words, the Prime Minister's office.

Other Protestant scholars admit it too, that when Jesus gives to Peter the keys of the kingdom, Peter is receiving the Prime Minister's office, which means dynastic authority from the Son of David, Jesus, the King of Israel, but <u>also an office where there will be dynastic succession</u>. When I discovered that, it was like the blinders fell off. Within a few weeks I had gotten together with the leading Protestant theologian in the world, one of the most reputable anti-Catholic Protestant theologians and spent ten hours with him and then in a Mercedes we drove two hours and I presented this case, and his only comment was, "that's clever." But he said, "you don't have to follow the Pope because of that." I said, "why not?" And he said, "Well, I'm going to have to think about it." He said, "I've never heard that argument before." And I said, "it' s one of the basic arguments that Cajeton used against the Protestants in the 16th Century and Cajeton was one of the most well-known defenders of the Catholic faith and you've never heard of him before?" I said, "I had never heard of it before until I discovered it on my own and then found it in all these other people." And he said, "That's clever." Clever, perhaps. True, definitely; enlightening, illuminating, very interesting.

Albright says some other things. "It is of considerable importance that in other contexts, when the disciplinary affairs of the community are discussed, the symbol of the keys is absent, since the saying applies in these instances to a wider circle. The role of Peter as steward of the kingdom is further explained as being the exercise of administrative authority as was the case of the Old Testament chamberlain who held the keys." Now, what he means there is that nowhere else, when other Apostles are exercising Church authority, are the keys ever mentioned. In Matthew 18, the Apostles get the power to bind and loose, like Peter got in Matthew 16, but with absolutely no mention of the keys. That fits perfectly into this model because in the king's cabinet, all the ministers can bind and loose, but the Prime Minister who holds the keys can bind what they have loosed or loose what they have bound. He has the final say. He has in himself the authority of the court of final appeal and even Protestants can see this.

In fact, Martin Luther in 1530, years after he had left the Church, wrote: "Why are you searching heavenward in search of my keys? Do you not understand, Jesus said, 'I gave them to Peter. They are indeed the keys of heaven, but they are not found in heaven for I left them on earth. Peter's mouth is my mouth, his tongue is my key case, his keys are my keys. They are an office.' They are a power, a command given by God through Christ to all of Christendom for the retaining and remitting of the sins of men." The only thing that Luther won't admit is that there was succession after Peter died, which is exactly what the keys denote, given their Old Testament background.

Gerhardt Meier, an Evangelical Protestant German scholar, wrote a famous book that conservative Protestants frequently refer to, "The End of the Historical Critical Method". In his article, "The Church and the Gospel of Matthew," Meier says [pages 58-60] "Nowadays, a broad consensus has emerged which, in accordance with the words of the text applies the promise to Peter as a person." This is a Protestant speaking now. "On this point liberal and conservative theologians agree," and he names several Protestant theologians from the liberal to the conservative side. "Matthew 16:18 ought not to be interpreted as a local church. The church in Matthew 16:18 is the universal entity, namely the people of God. There is an increasing consensus now that this verse concerning the power of the keys is talking about the authority to teach and to discipline, including even to absolve sins." Professor Gerhardt Meier is a Protestant with no interest in supporting the Catholic claim but, as an honest scholar, he admits that Peter is the one that Jesus is giving His power to. "Peter is the rock, and the keys signify, not only disciplinary power to teach, but even to absolve sins. With all due respect to the Protestant Reformers, we must admit that the promise in Matthew 16-18 is directed to Peter and not to a Peter-like faith. As Evangelical theologians, especially, we ought to look at ourselves dispassionately and acknowledge that we often tend unjustifiably toward an individualistic conception of faith. To recognize the authenticity of Matthew 16:17 ff. demands that we develop a Biblically based ecclesiology or doctrine of the church."

Gerhardt Meier is showing, as an honest scholar, that the church, which Jesus speaks of, is a universal church, not just a local congregation, another favorite ploy of anti-Catholic apologists. He says, "No, the church He's talking about is the one, holy, Catholic Church, the universal church and the rock on which it will be built is Peter, not Peter's confession. And the keys that Jesus gives to Peter are keys not only to teach, but even to absolve sins." Meier's not saying, they should all become Catholics, but what they should honestly do is to grant the Catholics the point because if they are honest in interpreting the Bible, they have to admit these conclusions.

Another Lutheran professor, a professor of scripture and theology at Concordia Seminary in Hong Kong, Torg Forberg wrote an article entitled, "Peter, High Priest of the New Covenant." Forberg insists that Jesus is the ultimate High Priest in the New Testament, but he says, "Peter is presented as some kind of successor to the High Priest in tradition used by the final redactorate, Matthew 16:13-19. Peter stands out as a kind of chief Rabbi who binds and looses in the sense of declaring something to be forbidden or permitted. Peter is looked upon as a counterpart to the High Priest. He is the highest representative for the people of God." This is Protestant testimony.

Elsewhere I found, in The Interpreter's Bible, "The keys of the kingdom would be permitted to the chief steward in the royal household and with them goes plenary authority, unlimited power, total. Post-apostolic Christianity is now beginning to ascribe to the Apostles the prerogatives of Jesus." The person who wrote this section in the Interpreter's Bible is saying, "I don't think personally that Jesus ever said these words. How could Jesus give to the Apostles prerogatives that are His own?" Well, the Church has always said that Jesus said this and what Jesus is giving is His own grace, His own power and His own authority to His Apostles.

Now Bultmann, one of the most notorious and well-known Protestant Biblical scholars of the century argues that it is impossible to regard Matthew 16 as an authentic saying of Jesus. He said, "How could He have envisioned the future development of an organized congregation of followers and appointed for them Peter as possessor of the power to teach and to discipline?" I have several other quotations here. I won't go through them all, but I will summarize with a quotation from an English Protestant scholar, J. N. D. Kelly in his book, *Oxford Dictionary of the Popes*. He says, "The Papacy is the oldest of all Western institutions with an unbroken existence of almost 2000 years."

Today scholarly dialogue is exciting, and some essential points are now being admitted and acknowledged by both sides. But still many Protestants, or non-Catholics, are so vehemently opposed to the Catholic Church, that they will return to the over-reaction of the Protestants, the anti-Catholic misinterpretations, and use them.

A good friend of mine in a recent debate with a Protestant minister who was using it right and left, even after the debates, went up to him and said, "Do you think, even though you are arguing that Peter isn't the Rock because you were quoting this and that and the other thing, do you think that Peter is the Rock?" And the anti-Catholic debater said, "Of course I do!" Although he had argued against that position, he held it himself. He just wanted to undermine the Catholic teaching. There is a broad consensus emerging, and it's a strong and sure foundation that can be built on in discussions and dialogues.

Common Objections to Papal Infallibility
Some common objections are: How could a human be infallible? Isn't infallibility a prerogative of God alone? Infallible? Teaching nothing but truth? To err is human, to forgive divine. You know we don't need infallibility. We can't have it. It isn't human.

We never say that the infallible Popes do not commit sin. They do. They are not impeccable; they are fallible as persons; they sin. As persons, they make mistakes. As persons, they might hold the wrong opinion inside their own minds; but Christ prevents them, through the Holy Spirit in His omnipotent love, from ever sitting down in the Chair of Peter and teaching the wrong opinions as Catholic beliefs. It's ultimately the infallibility of Christ that is the foundation for whatever we ascribe to the Popes.

First of all, if I were to sit down and write a textbook in Algebra, and a thousand proofreaders from across the world all went through it with a fine-tooth comb, and after years they didn't find a single mistake, would you have to conclude, "This was not written by a man, but by God because there are no mistakes?" No, of course not. I mean to err is human, but to be human is not to err only and always, continually. We can make mistakes, but we don't have to! And God can prevent us from doing so.

You hear Protestants says sometimes, like I always used to say, "You know this idea of infallibility just doesn't belong to humans." But then you think about it another minute. Non-Catholic Christians rarely admit that the Bible is infallible because the Biblical authors were given the gift of infallibility: Matthew, Mark, Luke, John, Peter, Paul, James, Jude - all of them wrote infallible truth. In fact, the Bible Christians insist that the Bible alone is our authority because the Bible is infallible.

Well, ask them: If God was capable of using thousands of sinners to infallibly communicate infallible truth so that the Church could see it as the truth, which is the Bread of Life, which is Christ himself and all the teachings… if God could do that, with fallible sinners, like Peter and Paul and John and Matthew, couldn't He still do it? In other words, certainly God is capable; and if you look around at how the Church spreads throughout the world, and how the Church encounters all kinds of crazies down through the ages, do you suppose that Jesus would say, "Well, once I give the Church this infallible scripture, there really is no need anymore for infallible interpretations of scripture. The Church can hold together just with the infallible Bible." Oh, really? In just 500 years, there are literally thousands and thousands of denominations that are becoming ever more numerous continuously because they only use the Bible. It points to the fact that we need an infallible interpretation of this infallible book.

Can you imagine the fathers of our country putting together the U.S. Constitution and mailing it out to every citizen and saying, "Fend for yourselves. Go it alone; with the spirit of Washington, you will be guided to your proper interpretation." What do you call that? Anarchy. We wouldn't have lasted a month as a nation. The Constitution established a governmental structure with a court of final appeal, the Supreme Court, which is final in all matters of constitutional interpretation. If the constitutional founders had sufficient wisdom to see the need for one little nation in 200 years to have a court of final appeal, how much more would Christ see the need to establish and constitute in the Church, (and put in His constitution) not only the truth but the official organs for interpreting, enforcing, explaining, preaching, and proclaiming that truth. It's just common sense. It's not unprecedented either.

Somebody could say, "Well, this idea of Peter speaking ex-cathedra, that's bogus, that's novel, that's unheard of." I would say, "No, it's not." When the Pope speaks from the Chair of Peter, ex cathedra, "from the seat" or "from the cathedra" ("cathedral" means the church where the bishop's cathedra or chair is) the Church is building on the teachings of Jesus. In Matthew 23:1-2, *Then said Jesus to the crowds and to His disciples, "The scribes and the Pharisees sit on Moses' seat. So practice and observe whatever they tell you, but not what they do, for they preach but they don't practice."* Later in Matthew 23, Jesus calls the scribes and Pharisees "fools, hypocrites, blind guides, vipers and whitewashed tombs." He doesn't think too highly of the scribes and the Pharisees. But what does He say in verse 1? "The scribes and the Pharisees sit on Moses' seat." Therefore, "you have to," it's in the imperative tense, "You have to practice and observe whatever they tell you." Whatever they tell you, you have to practice and observe. Why? Because they sit on Moses' seat. The Greek word is "cathedra". The Church, when it speaks of Peter's authority, i.e. Popes speaking ex-cathedra, is simply borrowing from Jesus' teaching.

I would challenge anybody to go back into the Old Testament and find some explicit text in the Old Testament where we find Moses establishing a chair, some endowed seat that will always have successors. You don't find a text explicitly saying that. So why does Jesus refer to it? Because there is also oral tradition, even in the Old Testament, which was used by God to transmit certain essential terms that the covenant family of God requires and depends upon for its life. Jesus doesn't quote a text. He appeals to a well-known oral tradition that He assumes the scribes and the Pharisees know about as well as His listeners. He doesn't just assume they know it, He assumes they are going to submit to it, and that they have been submitting to it. They have been experiencing problems because Old Testament priests and bishops are sometimes just as troublesome as New Testament priests and bishops are. But why do we follow? Because Jesus Christ established in the Old Testament a seat of Moses which is replaced in the New Testament with the seat of Peter.

The Old Testament doesn't have the full disclosure of all final revelation, but Jesus tells us that He will guide us in all truth in the New Testament. We don't say that Moses and his successors were infallible, because the fullness of the truth had not yet been given. But once it is given to the Apostles and their successors, we can see why Jesus guarantees that the gates of Hades will not prevail against the Church. Because of what Jesus has entrusted to this cathedra, this Petrine seat, the seat of Peter in Rome.

This is such assurance regardless of John XI or John XII, or Alexander VI, three of the most sinful Popes in all of history.

We have had scoundrels for Popes. It's amazing that there were really only three or four scoundrels, but even that number should bother you. But should it cause you to overthrow your confidence in listening to the successor of Peter, the Vicar of Christ, the Pope? No, of course not. For one thing, these scoundrels were too busy sinning to even attempt teaching from the seat of Peter. They didn't. Yet they brought great confusion upon the Church. But let's consider the fact that Jesus chose twelve Apostles, didn't He? And what about those twelve Apostles? One of them was Judas. Did Jesus know it before-hand? You bet He did. Why did He choose him? Maybe to get us ready for Judas priests in all generations.

Peter's Place in the Early Church

What does the Church do after Jesus is ascended into heaven, after Judas has committed suicide? In Acts 1:15, Peter stands up with the eleven in the Upper Room, and He speaks about Judas' death: *It was known beforehand and had even been prophesied in the Old Testament.* Notice that it is Peter who stands up. He's not just contributing an opinion. When Peter declares an opinion, it is binding and immediately followed. He quotes the Psalms, *Let his habitation become desolate and let there be no one to live in it.* But he doesn't say, "Hey, guys, we're from twelve down to eleven." He says, *His office, let another take.* Or, as the King James version says, *His bishopric, let other men take.* The word there is *episcopae*, from which we have the word *episcopacy* or *episcopal.* It's the word for bishop. In other words, there's an episcopal office that is now vacant. Peter stands up and, appealing to Old Testament prece-dent of patriarchal succession at every level in God's family, says "Let another man his bishopric, his office, take." The Old Testament practice was not just at top with Moses and his seed and his successors, but even the seventy elders, when they died, left empty offices that had to be filled. They draw lots and choose Matthias. No debate, no novelty. No, they understand, but even more, they submit. There's no debate, no discussion.

Notice also in Acts 2:14, Peter's responsibility, not just over the ten, but over all of Jerusalem. He is the one who preaches the first sermon. He is the spokesman for the Church to the world on the first Pentecost. Then in Acts 3 is Peter's second sermon. Peter is the instrument by which the first real healing miracle occurs, the lame man in the temple in Jerusalem in the portico called Solomon. In Acts 4, Peter's pre-eminence emerges even more as he exercises his teaching authority over the Jewish senate, the Sanhedrin. He's put on trial, but he comes to His own defense, putting the Sanhedrin itself on trial for crucifying the Lord. He exercises supreme authority over the Jewish senate. It left them flabbergasted! Who does this fisherman think he is? The Vicar of Christ over the family of God! And so they're set free. They are astounded at his boldness.

Then in Acts 5, Ananias and Sapphira, two wealthy members of the Church, sell some land and then lie about how much money they gave to the Church. Peter said to Ananias, "What are you doing?" Ananias says, "Well I gave you all the money." And Peter says, "You are lying to the Holy Spirit." Ananias said, "No, I'm just lying to you, Peter." But no. In lying to Peter, Ananias was lying to the Holy Spirit and to the Church. He's struck dead! A few hours later his wife Sapphira comes along. Peter says, "What happened?" "Oh, we sold the land for this amount, and we gave you all the money." And, "Hark, the footsteps of the men who just carried out your husband are coming for you." She drops dead! *And great fear came upon all those who heard of it.* [Acts 5:5] No wonder. Petrine promise was rather apparent here.

Peter's pre-eminence was on display for the whole Church, the whole world, and all the Jews to see and to behold. In Acts 8, for the first time non-Jewish half-breeds, Samaritans, are brought into the Church. They are baptized. Word reaches Jerusalem. Immediately, Peter and John go down there and give the sacrament of Confirmation. [verse 14] *When the Apostles in Jerusalem heard that Samaria had accepted the word of God, they sent Peter and John to them. When they arrived, they prayed they might receive the Holy Spirit.* They were baptized but they hadn't received this additional grace that we associate with Confirmation. Then the laying on of hands; they received the Holy Spirit and then Simon Magus tries to buy the gift and Peter rebukes him.

[verse 20] *May your money perish with you because you thought you could buy the gift of God with money. You have no part to share in this ministry because your heart is not right before God. Repent of this wickedness and pray to the Lord and perhaps He will forgive you for having such a thought in your heart, for I see that you are full of bitterness and captive to sin.* At this point Simon, who probably had heard of Ananias and Sapphira was trembling. He says, *Pray to the Lord for me so that nothing you have said may happen to me.* Even if some don't see Peter's promise, at least Simon Magus, the first heretic in the Church, did.

In Acts 11, the Gentiles, the swine, those that the Jews had often considered to be mere beasts come into the Church. Cornelius, the first Gentile believer is entering the Church. This is going to cause scandal. What's the Holy Spirit going to do? Have Peter be the first to authorize and admit the first Gentile Christian.

Peter has a vision, in Acts 10 and 11: he's being commanded by God in this vision to kill and to eat unclean animals that symbolize the Gentiles. He says, "I've never done it." Three times later he says, "Okay, okay, I'll do it." And then these people come and say, "We're being sent from Cornelius, the Gentile

Centurion." In a dream, in a vision, the Lord had said to Cornelius, "Send for a guy named Peter." Peter goes up to the house and says after baptizing Cornelius, *I now realize how true it is that God does not show favoritism but accepts men from every nation who fear him and do what is right.*

So then he goes ahead, preaches the gospel, baptizes these Gentiles and admits the first non-Jewish believers into the Church. This could have been the greatest crisis of all, but it isn't. In Acts 11:2, *When Peter went up to Jerusalem, the circumcised believers criticized him and said, "You went into the house of uncircumcised men and ate with them."* And Peter explained "Hey, God told me." It's Peter who says this, and criticism stopped.

The crisis reaches an even higher point in chapter 15:6-7. The famous Council of Jerusalem has a huge debate tearing apart the Church. These Gentile believers, do we circumcise them or not? Well you might say, "How important is that?" Well, if you were a man twenty through forty, considering conversion which meant circumcision, conversion might take a lot longer than if all that was needed was baptism, right? Notice, as the debate is raging, all of a sudden it stops. When? *After much debate Peter stood up and addressed them*, and he says the Holy Spirit purified their hearts through Baptism; circumcision isn't needed. End all debate! The only thing that follows is that James, the Bishop of Jerusalem, adds a kind of qualifying proviso so that the Jews are not needlessly scandalized in Gentile lands. But Peter's word was final and absolute. The debate ended. Peter had spoken.

Early Church Fathers Recognized Papal Primacy and Succession

Now you might say, "Well, this is just Peter." No, the keys symbolize succession. An office which is left vacant must be filled.

This is something that the Church understood. This is something that was well known to the early Church. The early Church, after the death of the last Apostles, recognized that the Bishop of Rome had Peter's authority and that that authority was final and absolute. Clement of Rome, about 96 A. D., writing to Corinth about this disunity, says "But if any disobey the word spoken by him, Peter, through us..." Remember Linus, Cletus, Clement, Sixtus? Those were the first Popes.

Irenaeus, writing in the 2nd Century, says, "Anyone who wishes to discern the truth may see in every Church in the whole world, the apostolic succession clear and manifest." We saw that in Acts 1. If Judas' office when left vacant is filled by a successor, then why should we be scandalized and lose our faith if a Pope is a scoundrel? You may say, "The Pope shouldn't be a scoundrel." I'd say, "yeah, amen." But Jesus knew that it wasn't going to be human strength and human authority that would put it all together for the Church. That's why He chose a Judas in the first place, to assure our hearts that no matter who was in the apostolic seat, whether it's Peter or the other Apostles, his Bishops, it's Jesus' omnipotent love for His family that will see us through to the truth, no matter what may come.

Irenaeus goes on and says, "We can enumerate those who were appointed as bishops in the churches by the Apostles and their successors down to our own day, but as it would be very long in a book of this kind to enumerate the successors of all through the churches, I will point out the Apostolic tradition in faith announced to mankind." And it goes on. Tertullian in the late 100's and the early 200's A. D. said, "Was anything withheld from Peter who was called the Rock on which the Church should be built, who also obtained the keys to the kingdom of heaven with the power of binding and loosing in heaven and earth?" Origen, in the late 100's spoke of Peter first because; "He was more honored than the rest." St. Cyprian spoke of the

Roman Church founded on Peter who fixed his chair in Rome. He speaks of the Church in Rome as our Mother Church, "the root of universality and Catholicity."

Hilary in the 300's speaks of the foundation of the Church on the Rock from which the Church was built. In other words, the early Church Fathers recognized this. The Protestant historian, Goodspeed, in his history book says, "The claim of primacy among the bishops for its head began under Victor in the 2nd Century and progressed under Calistus who claimed the power of the keys and reached a peak under Stephen in the 3rd Century, who professed to occupy the chair of St. Peter." Now even Cyprian, when he opposed Stephen as Pope, didn't oppose authority but opposed his opinions. Then finally, because Cyprian is St. Cyprian, he gave in to the Pope which is why he became a saint. St. Cyprian says, "A primacy is given to Peter, and it is thus made clear that there is but one Church and one Chair." The Syriac saint and Father, St. Ephraim, reaches to the clouds for words to describe the authority of Peter and his successors in the Sea of Rome.

I recommend a three-volume work written by Professor Jurgens, *The Faith of the Early Fathers*, which goes through all the Fathers and the many, many things they said to show that they recognize this authority in the Pope. Augustine, for instance, "Even if some traitor crept into this order of Bishops which is drawn from Peter, himself, up to Anastasius who now occupies the same See, he would not prejudice the Church." He speaks of the *cathedre Petri*. St. Augustine, a great saint and Father that the Protestants revere, had more things to say about the Popes as successors to Peter with all of his plenary authority than almost anybody else in the first seven centuries of the Church. He said, "Who is ignorant that the chief Apostolate is to be preferred to any Episcopate?" Of the dignity of Peter he says, "in whom the primacy of the Apostles shone forth with excelling grace."

Now, we could go on and on. Somebody could say, "Now, wait a second. Why wasn't Papal infallibility defined until the 1800s? The Bible never says Papal infallibility." No it doesn't. But the Bible never says Trinity, either. And all non-Catholic Christians affirm the Trinity. Why wasn't the word "Trinity" used? Well, because the word Trinity wasn't necessary until heresies arose that forced the Church to formulate and to defend the doctrine of God, one God in Three Persons, adequately and sufficiently. At that point, they came up with a very helpful term, "Tri-unity" or Trinity to do so. Likewise, in looking at Matthew 16 and the unconditional guarantee that Jesus gives to Peter, the recipient of the keys, that the gates of Hades will not prevail against the Church which is built upon the Rock. The gates of Hades will not prevail against Peter and his successors. Well, the gates of Hades derive their power from error, from untruth, from falsehood, the father of lies. If one lie is allowed into the Church's pure, sacred teaching, that's like taking a windowpane and putting one crack into it. I'll tell you what happens. I was driving down a highway in Milwaukee and a little pebble bounced up and just touched the windshield, a little crack. What happened? Over the next few months that crack grew and grew, and the windshield had to be replaced because the whole thing could have shattered.

If one should admit one falsehood, defined as truth, the gates of Hades have prevailed. Christ has given us an unconditional guarantee that they will not prevail because he will build His Church upon Peter and His successors, the Rock, the foundation stone. This gives us confidence because the family of God on earth is never left without a father figure to teach and to help us.

Now, if a Judas-type occupies the Chair, you better believe that God will graciously pour out an extra measure of the Holy Spirit to protect His children and see that that scoundrel is out, quick. And they were. Every Catholic historian will admit that certain Popes, a very, very few, were acting too much like scoundrels to even bother teaching, thanks be to God. But even this gives to us the kind of confidence we need as God's sons and daughters to listen to the Holy Father, John Paul II. In the Pope, we hear the voice of Christ because of this awesome grace that is given to the Pope, one of the many graces that Christ died to give to us.

Let's treasure it. Let's cherish it and let's live it out with God's grace and power.

More About Scott Hahn

Catholic theologian and best-selling author Dr. Scott Hahn, Ph.D. was formerly a Presbyterian minister. Prior to his conversion to Catholicism, Dr. Hahn was a militant opponent of the Catholic Church - a "Bible-believing" evangelical who thought the Catholic Church should be publicly denounced.

Since being received into the Church in 1986, his powerful conversion testimony has become the most widely distributed Catholic audiotape of all time.

Because of his detailed knowledge of both Scripture and of Protestant theology, Dr. Hahn has become a most effective advocate for the truth of the Catholic Church, and he is considered to be one of the most inspirational Catholic theologians and biblical scholars in the United States.

Dr. Hahn has had several #1 best-selling books in the category of Catholic non-fiction and was named "The leading author of Catholic hardcover books" for 2002 by the Catholic Book Publishers Association.

Currently, Dr. Hahn is Professor of Biblical Theology at the Franciscan University of Steubenville, Ohio and the Director of the St. Paul Center for Biblical Theology. With the motto "Reading the Bible from the Heart of the Church," the St. Paul Center maintains a website (salvationhistory.com) with many helpful resources, a weblog, Bible study tools and more.

The "Why Stay Catholic?" series of books is adapted from Dr. Hahn's best-selling audio series, "Answering Common Objections" produced by St Joseph Communications.

For more information on the many books, videos, cassettes and CDs by Dr. Hahn available from St. Joseph Communications call toll-free **800.526.2151** or order on-line at **www.saintjoe.com**.